Maybe Street

Maybe Street

Selected Poems of Anna Buck

Acknowledgements

Maybe Street is the main street of Bombala, NSW.
Many thanks to Anna's family, especially her husband Bob.

Maybe Street: Selected Poems of Anna Buck
ISBN 978 1 76109 097 4
Copyright © this selection with introduction and notes
Tim Metcalf 2021
Copyright © poems and cover artwork Anna Buck 2021

First published 2021 by
GINNINDERRA PRESS
PO Box 3461 Port Adelaide 5015
www.ginninderrapress.com.au

Contents

Introduction

Anna used to joke that she was 'the most successful unsuccessful writer I ever knew'. In 2004, she was shortlisted for the Newcastle prize with her poem 'Maybe Street'. By 2006, she had appeared three times in the annual *Best Australian Poems* anthology. In 2008, she appeared there for the fourth time. In the same year, she came second in the Rosemary Dobson award, and second (for a short story entitled 'Maybe Street') in the prestigious Josephine Ulrich prize. She was for the fourth time shortlisted for the Newcastle Poetry Prize ('The Butcher-bird'), and was joint winner of the NSW Poet's Union prize ('In the Clearing'). She was in touch with Les Murray and one step from the top when serious illness intervened. Her poetry CV ended in the same year that it peaked.

Anna loved Australia. She loved the bush and the endless stories it generates. In this, she differs from many of our poets: her experience was not visited – a superficial day out from the city – it was lived, and profoundly so. Some of her work recalls her childhood, but most of it is based in the Bega Valley Shire, where she lived for many years: in Bombala, Rocky Hall, Wyndham, Pambula, Candelo and Bega.

She was born in southern England in 1948. The family decided to emigrate, as 'ten-pound Poms', and her parents found themselves multitasking in an isolated Aboriginal community on the NSW north coast. Contact with the Indigenous people of this country will usually leave a profound and indelible impression upon the genuine poet: Anna often spoke fondly of this time in her life.

Her husband Bob recalls that she wrote every day, occasionally under a pseudonym; she also helped a lot of people start writing. She wrote, for example, about 120 poems, 1,500 'Annagrams' for the Bega paper, children's stories, a memoir and two plays.

'She was multi-talented as a visual artist as well as a writer,' affirms Nance Cookson, an exuberant Ginninderra Press poet. 'Anna was a generous spirit in so many ways. She was president of the regional Fellowship of Australian Writers, and if Anna looked over your work, you were fortunate indeed, for it seemed that with a magic wave of the hand she could transform an ordinary poem or story into something extraordinary.'

Another long-term poetry associate, Alexandra Seddon, described her friend in 2018: 'There are those who give like a tree in a valley, just giving out these blossoms into space, not even thinking that it is giving, and that's Anna.'

Ever the storyteller, many of her poems are entertaining vignettes in which present and past reverberate. Her narrative style shifts in time, but is not 'postmodern'. She is conversational, rarely formal (though she admired the great English canon). Perhaps her childhood contact with Aboriginal people helped her develop this certain ideological freedom from the schoolwork poetry of her post-war homeland.

Unlike most, Anna understood freedom as 'being' in nature, not as piling up possessions. She wrote that she had 'an idyllic childhood in a succession of derelict mansions and farm labourer's cottages, with a focus on the natural world around us and the beauty of life'. Life for her is an ongoing experience of endless creativity; and chaos, not imposed order, is the way of the universe of understanding. Flowers in her poetry are allowed to be themselves: they wilt, and the dead and dying compost to nourish the new. If she writes about the richness and variety of domestic life in the bush, there is always a bite: there is always a huge fruit bat hanging like a wrecking ball in the orchard. Anna is never simplistic or sentimental. She has done this rural women's work herself.

A wry humour forms the pervasive tone of Anna's many poems about rural Australia. She combined an English quirkiness and an Australian dryness with an acute eye for the incongruous or absurd. She preferred detail to sweeping vistas or endless skies. She was drawn to the broken and irrational things of this world, as if those things, like the odd people of the bush, could not sit still in inanimate perfection. Something was always breaking, or being undone. The domestic compromises that the bush pushes us into, that frustrate then lead many people to despair, Anna assimilated into her world. She carried on chuckling at the cracks in perfection rather than retreating back into a neat and tidy self-imposed urban domesticity.

'Anna's writing is as honest, observant and understated as the woman herself. She was a master of the craft, whose reflections on her life and the places she lived it are simultaneously funny and moving,' says Candelo poet Monique Watt.

Anna's hesitation to put together a collection something like this originated, she said, in her being never quite sure a given poem was finished. It was a struggle to call a major piece completed and send it away to a journal or a competition. Anna also used to say that she did not think of herself as a poet. Her reticence was such that when in 2018 she agreed to let me help her, I understood that she was acknowledging she was soon to leave us.

Her poems flowed seamlessly when read in her clear voice,

and the reader who wishes to hear her can do so on the internet audio project Poets of the Bega Valley Shire. The full collection of Anna's poems is held by the Buck family in Bega. Her publication details can be found inside Trove at the National Library of Australia.

Anna was always working on her poems. Just as with reality, she was never blinded to imperfections. The poems published here are all the last drafts approved by her. In the few places where her natural diction does not translate well to the page, to avoid an occasional ambiguity or lost sense, I have added punctuation. Uncommon terms are elucidated in footnotes. I have selected and arranged the poems in a way that I hope Anna would approve.

Writing this, I pause to look down and across town. Maybe Street is the main street, on the other side of the river here in Bombala, NSW. Months ago, the valley was filled with dense smoke from bushfires. Now it is filling with frost and hearth-smoke. Either way, Anna would have delighted in the echidna strolling down Dickinson Street, past the Catholic church on the left and the police residence on the right, apparently on its way to Maybe Street, like the rest of us.

Tim Metcalf
Bombala, NSW, 2018–2020

Two out of Ten

When they took away the schoolhouse
wisteria straddling the veranda
fell, its back broken
showering blue petals and bees
into hydrangeas acidic with tea leaves
teachers' wives had thrown there
since 1851.

It took a front-end loader,
two trucks, a day
and four smokoes
to break the house in three
and haul bloodwood slabs
and corrugated iron away.

When the cortège passed
rooms where children had lain
(scraped knees or headache eased
by aspirin and blowfly hum;
clean knickers handed out,
hollow teeth painted with clove oil)
were exposed; shadowy
corners sliced as if by the Blitz.

French doors flapped.
The chalk dust ghost
realising dispossession
sought to haunt
stone steps leading up
to nothing.

The whiskered lemon tree
with nowhere to hide
wept little green fruit
bitterly, took a
detention, forgot its lunch
stood outside
for the rest of the century.

Mother's Day

I listened to Mother's Day stories
on the radio and thought of you,
tipsy by the front gate in the moonlight,
giggling and lighting matches
with your boyfriend to see glow worms by.

Later Dad picked you up,
put you over his shoulder
and carried you as far as the well
where you suddenly became too heavy
so he sat you on the rim
and went to open the back door,
took himself inside, locked it
and went back to bed.

In the warm summer night
you beat on its boards
with your hands whispering
so as not to wake Mrs Randall
Tom, Tom, let me in! and Dad
thought there was a moth
on the windowpane and looked
out to see your white face upturned;
I thought I forgot something, he said.

Essence

Dad's filing cupboard was painted
magenta because Grandad had
a tin of the stuff that needed using up.

Opened it released a wave of tobacco
in tins, a smell that hung around
his best green cardigan.

Packets of cabbage and radish seed
were filed with school reports and
letters saying we had run away from home,
had an abortion, were broke.
We never wrote to say we were happy.

Notebooks filled in italic script
with timetables and songs that
the children in his class might sing.

Peach and pear wine in flagons
clear as medicine and tasting like Wartkil
but all neatly labelled they were there for years
glowing like bedside lamps.

Underneath, in a space for a briefcase,
were his slippers, woollen tartan, lumpy
where his corns pushed out the fabric, thick with dust.

Renters flogged off the cupboard after Mum died.
Somewhere somebody opens a door
and gets a waft of Dad.

Splitting hares

from *Scandal*

Mum could make a meal out of dandelions
as long as her poacher pals or the keeper
slipped her rabbit, hare, pheasant, quail –
still warm in the sack, slapped on the table,
her carnivore's smile and auburn curls
enough reward; Dad liked to think his skill
as pub pianist was paid for in game and beer.
It's a disgrace, hissed wives from the Snug;
her a teachers wife, too – while at the bar
their gaffers sang along with Mum
and banged their mugs for more.

With her potato peeling knife she slit
through fluff between the hare's legs,
still twitching from his dawn leap
in the cowslip fields; spilled nets of gut
as intricate as Grandma's braids
onto the newspaper Mum had spread.
My brother could barely reach to see,
just on eye level with such butchery,
to check it was not his pet pheasant cock,
he who strutted beneath the beeches,
feathers a flash of copper among leaf mulch.

Despite the reproach in our faces
Mum stripped skin back with gypsy ease
chopped the naked hare through at the neck
said this is good clean kill. When I was small
my mother used to send me up the road
for block ornaments – great big cow bones,
stripped of every scrap of meat. She'd
boil them up for stock – white soup, we called it.
When it cooled we'd pick the blobs of fat off
suck it as if it was chocolate, a treat.

Later, with blood, skin, sinew, gut, head
all spirited away, except the powder puff
with which our baby sister played,
the soft meat and herbs teased our taste buds.
We blanked out the memory of the smear, red
as Mum's lipstick, on the hare's mouth,
which made it look as though it smiled.

Scandal

The butcher's wife had a nose
that turned blue in winter; her face
otherwise white, stretched too tight
over sharp bones; her hands red
from scrubbing the counter.
She served dark purple mince,
wrapped it in white paper.
In the background shapes hung
and swung, bled into sawdust.
The butcher's face was mottled
like flowering bruises and solid
as the corpses in the cool room.
His cleaver came down with finality,
chopped sinew, bone and muscle
through at one stroke. His mastery
at reducing beasts to Sunday
dinner chunks a joyless art;
His daughters lead him a merry dance,
Mum said – another reason why
he never smiled and seldom spoke –
except when he handed me soft parcels
that seeped and pushed his face into mine –
when's your mother going to settle her bill?
Our lack of funds the reason I was sent.

Once, dawdling on this bloody errand,
I pushed my face into the fence
that adjoined the dairy. Here,
the only thing to fear was the quick-
eyed collie who would lick my face
but turn on my heels and nip.
Slowly, on legs guided by habit
the cows came into the yard,
udders leaking in anticipation
of relief from the machine
that took the place of butting calf.
They went straight to their stalls,
breathed mist over churns and crates,
the warm smell of hay and the sound
of their cud-chew as comforting
as the suck and hiss of milk.

One eye-hole away was the butcher's
backyard, the concrete here stark
in late afternoon's winter light.
Through a gap in the slats
I saw a cow stand, her teats trailed
near the ground. The butcher's wife
had her arms wrapped around
the animal's neck, held it tight.
The butcher put what looked like
a hose against the cow's head.
She lifted it once, and snorted,
a last attempt to throw off those
who harassed her, return to
the anonymity of the herd.
The bang, not loud, yet powerful
made a round hole in her skull.
Her eyes rolled up, she slewed,
her legs buckled and she sank.
Her captor stepped aside with skill,
as though woman and cow
were locked in a bizarre tango.

There was no meat on our table that night,
and I could never say why I had failed.
Mum supposed our credit had been stopped,
and cursed the butcher for refusing a child.
One of his girls slept with an airman
and brought forth, defiant, a baby,
to be walked in a pram with high wheels.
She's as lovely as her mum, mine said,
generous against the lash of scandal,
she'd felt it hard against her own heels.

She peeked in at the butcher's granddaughter
who struggled against ribbon and knitted lace;
I looked too, and saw the colours
of the slaughter-yard in that squashed face.

from Worshippers (Part 3)

The Hicks kids don't just blaspheme
they shout strange guttural words
and have seen their father pull calves
out of cow's backsides, blood mixing with manure.
We have never heard such words before
and wait for a reaction as the last round of curses
echo around the graveyard.
Mr Hicks sticks his head out of the cottage –
if you kids don't stop that swearing
I'll tan your bloody arses for you!

Their mother sends them out to picnic
on the tombstones; they clutch lumps
of pink sausage meat, suck it out the skins
like ice cream into which their noses run.
They will eat anything except yew berries
these they offer us in their palms like treats
to see if they can tempt us into nightmare sleeps;
then run home, snatch dog biscuits from a sack
crunch up crumbs of bone and mutton fat.

Hicks girls wear their mother's skirts with holes cut –
their arms poke through scarecrow style;
boy's pants are safety-pinned to their vests.
Mrs Hicks boils up the wash in her copper
tips in a packet of dye, starts with a light colour.
For a while the kids are streaked pale yellow
or blue, turn mauve, orange or green
as their clothes stain. At Harvest Festival
they come to church in deep purple
like members of a sect as their mother sets
a tin of pineapple chunks against the font.
By the time the elms are bare they are all in black
mourning the death of that particular batch.

Smile

1

she ran down the middle of the road
her mother told her she must to dodge
the flashers unzipped in dark alleys
her stockings slipped from bloomer
leg   shoes tapped a dance over
cobblestones her mouth crashed
down on picture postcard rounds
smashed her two front teeth   went home
concussed to clove poultices but
the jolt had gone to root   abscessed
she felt the choking sweetness of the mask
awoke to lick the bloody gap in gums
false teeth at nine   the dentist said
make her wear them all the time she'll
soon forget they're in her head

2

her laugh attracted dad strong
white teeth that split her face
she knew the world could bite and
teased it into submission
his sister and mother said *beware*
of small women they prey on tall men
and take their money please
don't bring her here again
he said *fine I won't come back either*
at the wedding she smiled in a green suit
short to show the shape of her calves
though there was plenty of silk in a parachute
the old ones clicked their tongues
when her man was sent away they knew
the bad luck colour had done it
stationed out of Sheffield he
missed the bombs his turn came through
desert years three times his tank was blown
from beneath him but he learnt to drink red
wine   he missed her laugh   maybe if they'd
had that time together he would have found
out sooner   came home on leave unexpected
found her front teeth in a cup beside the bed
married for two years before he knew
her teeth were not her own asked her did
her wooden leg unscrew felt the warmth
of her curled into his flesh
the secret of her imperfection
his alone to explore

3

as my mother chewed on cloves
and pressed hot water bottle to her face
while feeding nappies through the wringer
plans to tear down her home and place
the schoolmaster, his wife and seven
kids in grey concrete semi-detached
on the Oxford Road – a household
divided with two front paths – went ahead
a woman in twinset, pearls and perm knocked
on the doomed door showed her
an article saying God was good and said
there's a council house for everyone in heaven

mum said if that was the case she'd
rather go to hell   we emigrated instead
kids inspected   jabbed   approved
farmed out when the furniture went
a bit at a time   carried off up the road
she had her tooth out on the National Health
its clawed roots defied the dentist
she found herself lying on a bed
in a dark green corridor
from the purple and brown bruises
flowering down jaw and breast
she reckoned the surgeon stood on her chest
and had a clear memory of him shimmering
in the ether holding up a bloody trophy
saying *these aren't human*
they belong on a horse

25

while dad packed his books into kitbags
she doped herself with codeine
and tried to gather enough clothes
for six weeks on board
grey army blankets and a canteen
of cutlery from grandfather
her inheritance for the land down under
on the day we left
gathered in from billets
the lime trees on the green were rimed*
from root to twig and so was the line
of nappies in the schoolhouse garden
left for the thaw or bulldozers
mum's frozen flags of surrender
dry those if you can you bastards
it won't be heaven where I'm going
but Hell or Australia the sun might shine

* frosted

4

when a tooth broke off her set
she went without until the pension allowed
another the right shade of tobacco
and tea to match the front two an the molars
that went – one for each child, old wives said
should have been seven but her
hooked roots kept hollow shells firm

a habit of half-dropping the plate
in her open mouth made it
strange to see a smile on two levels
a black gap between her generous lip
and top teeth clicked up quickly at
her grown-up children's disapproval

living alone, she had no need to hide
their falsity they came out every night
and sometimes in daylight
never in the same place twice, she filed
them away in pantry dresser fridge
long searches at morning tea so she
could have a biscuit groping hands
on the mantelpiece you never knew
where her smile would turn up

when they were gone for one week two
stretching into three she resigned herself
to forking out on a new set her chum
from across the way stopped to chat
mum leaned over the veranda
in the morning sun puffed on her fag
her smile lopsided conversation lisped
friend reached into the greenery
plucked a pink and brown blossom
they'd been set on the rail to dry
and the cat   who liked that spot too
had knocked them into the geraniums

mum's smile was picked out studded
with red petals stuck on with frost smelling
sharp with crushed leaves silvered with snail trails
her delight a gappy beam laughter ringing out
I hear it now on the thin air dancing over tin
roofs and brown paddocks clear to the hills

5

she kept asking for her teeth in hospital
her bag followed her around
they didn't catch up with her before
we put her in the ground I wanted to
put them on her grave a centrepiece
for the roses and delphiniums
mum wouldn't have minded
she'd have known where they were

Southampton Docks

No day trip to the seaside
this concrete grey, sky and water meeting;
no rolling up of trouser cuffs or paddling:
the ship's hull towers, uninviting.

Mingled hope, fear and resignation on
migrant's faces muffled in November mist.
Ten pounds each is what they're worth,
exiles on one-way tickets
to a new life, not knowing that
the old life walks up the gangplank too.

They bring (in cardboard boxes,
canvas kitbags, bruised suitcases)
army blankets, button boxes, baby clothes.
Inside their disappointed bodies
bits of England have wedged themselves;
homesick screw worms spiralling
to surface, primrose pale
blinking in eucalyptus sunshine.

Swimming

down the dirt track to Lane Cove
the Shipley boys strip off their shirts
jump in the brown river, pedalling
imaginary bikes as they fall   shorts
balloon out around skinny brown legs
they come up blowing water out their noses

bull sharks comes up as far as the weir so
swim on this side a man was ate a month ago
there was all blood in the river you could see
him opening his mouth to shout for help
only no sound come out because he
was only half there he had no lungs

their sister smiles as she tells the English kids
white skinned and fat from six weeks on the ship
a kindness to stop the Poms slipping into salt
thrashing on the surface like fish food

they look at the wide water, grow pink in the sun
couldn't sharks shimmy over at high tide?
perhaps they'll eat the Shipley's first
slide down the stone bank toes sink in mud
once in they're forced to swim   soup up
to their necks the smell of all that has lived
and died there filling noses and mouths

kick out feel the cool of deep underneath
the lazy current tug at their legs
taking them towards the concrete spillway
then a clutch that grips and pulls the English
girl down she opens her mouth wonders will
any sound come out

as her cry bounces from the rocks
the boys surface beside her
white teeth grinning as fiercely as any sharks

Fleas

1

December rain blown up
from Lane Cove River
in gusts
lifting washing,
wet flags strung
between wooden huts.
Orange boxes crack as
fire in fuel stove takes
blue 'Mil' going into flames first,
'dura'* on the next bit
snapped over Dad's knee
to feed soup and citrus steam.

Youse 'ave got a sauna in 'ere,
she grins from the door,
baby on her hip unsmiling.
Sits herself down on chrome and vinyl,
'good' chairs rusting already
where the legs meet the seat.
What're youse tryin' to do,
suffocate the fleas?

* Mild…ura: an orange-growing town in Victoria

Glass of water at Dad's elbow
for drowning, parasite tea.
We wait, anticipate
he'll drink it
instead of sweet
brown muscat,
when he does
swallow our glee.

What are ya, a pair of old derros?
she asks the first time a sticky glass
is offered. *We drinks beer*
or tea over 'ere.
Or water?
Nah. Water's for washin.
Or mixin' with Condy's.
Condy's Crystals. *
Paint it on the boards.
Fleas don't like the smell.

* Condy's Crystals: potassium permanganate

Rae's* a veteran
of infestations,
iron hut a grey tank loaf.
Four kids under
corrugations
bake in January
freeze in July,
deafened in downpours.
*They saves the worst ones
for us*, she laughs at Mum's concern.
Cook us if they can't breed us out.

Well ah wouldn't stand for it Loov,
broadened vowels and
extra aspirants
meet somewhere in the common tongue
of women making the best of it.

* Rae: Aunty Rae Stuart

2

Yoonited Nations!
Rae flips up a whip
of blue-black hair
at daks and string vests,
soiled flags at half mast,
drooping in the summer damp.
Dutch woman's bloomers
sit on the line
wet or fine
hidey holes
for sand fleas
she won't
iron out the hems
cremate them in little patches
of brown blood, scratches
her way around the camp.

Rae doesn't hang
her shifts on display
strings her washing
out the back
doesn't want to catch
other people's fleas.

Mum tries to guess
her etymology
So tall and straight
that Roman nose –
if only she had teeth
is she a Pakistani?
Are Afghans allowed?

Rae shakes with wheezy
laughter when she hears
asthma and aitches
brought out by humidity.
HI'm a haboriginal,
she parodies
Han horiginal
Horstralian;
the honly black faces
you're likely to see
round 'ere.

3

Rae has a TV,
our payment
for minding her kids.
The tank smells of pea-
nut butter paint
and Condy's Crystals.
Don't sit on the chairs
Claudie's been pain-
tin' 'em again.
Don't sit on the settee,
either, unless you wants
to spend all night scratchin'.
Damn things 'ave got to go
somewhere I s'pose.

They sit cross-legged
around the screen
as if it were a campfire
eyes solemn in its glow
watching the Corona
girl sway her hips
so sparkelling a ling –
refreshering ering –
curls a blonde bouncing
sausage, pale pink
lipstick makes her mouth
indistinct
in black and white.

Toddler keens,
movie queen
not making up
for Rae's bony chest.
Change the channel instead
sandwich plugs the moan,
paste clagging soft white bread,
then bubby swallows, pushes head
into her sister's belly,
cries through the cushion.
Singer can't 'Twist and Shout'*
the wailing out.

*Will she sleep if I
lie her on the bed?'
Nah. She wants her twin.*
Through 'Shake Baby Shake'
turned up loud to drown the din
she tells how
the girls got gastro.
Rae carried the sickest through
Lindfield to the doctors'
came back breathless
for the other
found her empty,
fluids seeped away,
body collapsed
into the coverlet.
She died here?

* a Beatles song

Teeth stop in mid-masticate
we look at the bed
see the dint of a
small weight
life fluctuating
try to comprehend
while rain and singer
reverberate.

What're y' watchin' old
Johnny O'Keefe for?
He's madder'n a two-bob bit
takes four to hold him down
when he takes a fit.
Wet Rae holds her arms out
survivor scrambles up her,
a possum scaling a tree,
looks for
the counterbalance,
hides in the hollow of her neck.

4

Back past the washing
sun comes out, steam
rises off the Dutch woman's bloomers.
In our hut the fire has gone down,
soup baked hard in the bottom
of the pan. Mum stands in the doorway
smoking, Dad picks another flea
off his leg and watches it drown.

The Butcher-bird

1

Bets are laid at the pub as to
whether the van will get over
the log and plank bridge to the reserve.
Odds are on the Irish driver
ending up in the creek with our load;
after a few schooners they persuade him
to fall into a bed on the veranda
and do the road in daylight.

The Department hadn't reckoned on
Dad saying yes to a post up north
mozzies are as big as magpies up there
says his Head but we help the driver
carry the exploded settee out,
catch and box camp kittens
don't let them loose in the sleeper
until the train starts, out of sight
when the guard comes round.

Where's the bus to Bellbrook? Dad asks
while we huddle round the station fire.
They inspect his chit then call him two taxis
because we won't fit into one.
Thank God we're not paying for this!
As we are driven between mountains and river
dust seeps through the cab's vinyl;
then we climb and crest and far below
see small white houses tucked
well away from town.

We wait for our goods until dark falls
then break into the clinic and raid bags
sent by ladies in Warringah;
cover ourselves in nylon florals
huddle together on the boards.
The residents don't know the new manager
and matron are camping like a mob from Kyogle.

They come out to look from the huts
no bigger than the van, which sways
over the ruts; the driver is sheepish
when he sees us shiver still wrapped
in charity. Dad and the boys take the other end
as he shoves bits of our migrant life
into the frosty air, runs his fingers through
black curly hair wonders who
will be looking after who.

2

Coral trees border the driveway
orange/red blooms great spots of blood
leaves coming later when frosts
have finished; petals fall on a tennis court
as foreign as the notion that Dad is boss.
We think we are in paradise as a bird
breaks into a song more sweet and strong
than we have ever heard.

Children creep into the garden
steal the first of the strawberries
their stained mouths give them away
when the handyman shouts say
just lookin' for mully grubs to go fishin'!
He throws them out he knows they have no rods
poised on the bank, brown cranes they slice
river mullet in two with pieces of tin.

In the first week Ivy's little girl dies.
She stopped smiling a while ago
round face swollen with nephritis.
Mum, as matron, counts out pills
grainy, the colour of the worms they kill.
The children stand in line, crunch them
with Vegemite sandwiches
washed down with powdered milk.

Dad has the men plough the common
around which the huts curl, plant corn
spears bolt skywards, swelling along the stems.
Silk tassels tickle small heads as they hide
in the green, strip away husks, bite into rows
of milky pearls. Not one cob makes it to the table.
Later a bull pushes his way through flattens
the lot, children swing laughing on his tail.

All summer the song rises from the trees;
when the leaves start to fall Dad sees thorns
on which pieces of torn lizard are impaled.
A baby brown snake writhes, beetles kebabs for
the butcher-bird who fixes him with a wise eye
pure notes an aria. Years later in another life
Dad hears how too many worm pills fed to
rickety kids can make their kidneys fail.

3

The reserve kids cram into the back of Dad's EH
bounce over the track to Bellbrook where
a double-decker rises out of the mist beside the pub.
Lyall pours ether into the engine to get it to cough
they breathe in the fumes that flood the bus;
teachers question a lack of attention *we do what*
we can with these children but it's never enough.

Past Yurullgurra where the Conns get on
it's girls upstairs boys down where Lyall
can keep an eye on them no one ever says
where the reserve kids should sit, they never shift
from the bench seats near the door. Red dust drifts in
through windows and floor but always worst just there –
on dry days they disappear and in the frost they freeze.

The bus pulls in at Willawarrin on the return trip
picks up papers and bread, white high-tops charred
and crisp from sticking against the top of the brick oven.
Boxes displace the reserve kids – the smell of warm bread
on a July night too much for the Conns and Kesbys
who want to sit up the back and strip
the chewy black away from the loaves.

When the wet hits a jinker* driver loses his gears
coming over the ridge – brakes won't grip, his lights
blaze at the bus on the cutting. There's nowhere
to go but into the rock face. They climb out, leave it
resting on its side, slide in the mud, blind with rain.
Hold hands, shouts Lyall. *Smile, you dark kids, so
I can see you!* Herds them away from the edge.

United in a chain they resist the camber that would
tip them in the Macleay; slither clasped together
miles to the pub where shouts of laughter from the bar
say parents have not wasted time in worry.
Publican's wife comes out of the smoke, looks past them,
says *Damn kids have been at the bread again.*
Hands loosed they separate, once more invisible,
slide into the EH's back seat and wait.

*

* a heavy logging vehicle

4

Willie comes to the clinic for cough mixture
every inward breath a bagpipes tune.
Mum succumbs to his lanky charm –
you should see someone about those wheezes.
He smiles slowly, lifts his gaze to hers
*No, missus, no – not until I see that little man
sat on my chest grinning, when I see him
they can stick their needles into me then.*

The grazier wants the best stockmen
tells Dad to make sure Willie keeps away
from the pub the day before a muster.
Willie's eyes sink into the shadows
as Dad suggests he saves his energies
but you can see a gleam and the twist to his lips
as he agrees he won't walk over there today.
When McIntyre comes by cracking his whip
Willie has vanished on the dawn breeze.

·

He turns up that night at our back door
spouting from a bottle cut.
Ellen presses on the fountain
Mum adds her weight in the back seat
as Dad skates down the mountain
hopes Willie has enough blood to last
until they get to hospital he reckons
it's well thinned with alcohol.
Can you see the little man, Willie?
A chuckle from the rear
Yes, boss, but he's not grinning yet.

Mr Scott, Matron takes him to her chest
How have you managed to cut yourself?
Willie's skin is the shade of the ghost gums
but he turns his smile on her solid bust;
I was having a cup of tea with my wife
and I leaned back to get a cup and put
my hand through the cabinet glass.
She clicks her tongue, hugs him to her starch
leads him away for Dettol and stitches.

Dad helps him in when they get back
Willie seems to slip away from his hold
the bandage on his wrist a torch in the dark hut
where there is one table and an orange box.
Tell the missus I'm sorry I bled on her dress.
Ellen slides in behind him, the door is shut.

McIntyre rides up, his horse rolls the whites
of its eyes, does a sideways dance
Couldn't you keep him off the piss?
Inside the clinic Mum puts clean lint
on the wound, hears the hooves, her face
is close enough to feel the rise and fall
of Willie's ribs, says *you must take more care.*
Don't worry about me, missus, he smiles,
if the big man don't get me the little one will.

5

When the fire comes through the people take bits of tin
and sit by the creek. While the town truck pees on flames
and McIntyre's men beat burning grass with wet sacks
they slice the head off mullet and cook a good feed.

They are surprised at Dad's suggestion they should try
to save the huts. Leslie has already burnt his back fence
for firewood but a few of the men raise themselves and appease
the need to fight for painted fibro and stainless steel sinks.

Dad and Johnny and Ronnie Kelly sweat, put in a break
at the back of Willie's hut, Dad thinking of when his youngest
didn't come home after playing with Gladys there and he
    found her
curled up on the floor under coats, cockroaches crawling over
    the pair.

48

After that Gladys slept at the house sometimes until Ellen
    came down
and reclaimed her own, standing her ground. Mum hadn't
    known
this was the way the children went in the guise of care to
    clean sheets
in dormitories; nothing Mum said could reassure.

Let the bloody place burn. Dad puts his bad leg up on a chair
pours his firefighters a beer; they sip, uneasy, not liking
to say they are church elders and don't drink on Sunday
but the boss is a good bloke and they won't hurt his feelings.

Drum Roll

Seven drops on a cigarette paper*
that's when the men stop work
sit on their Eskies
cook crumpets on a shovel
over the tailings fire
in the lee of the Portaloo.

Seven drops fell yesterday
hit the Perspex with a crash
that sent the cats running,
round-eyed over shoulders;
then the snow clouds puckered,
a cow drawing up her udders.

All road workers
leaning on shovels
pretending to patch up potholes
should, at a given moment,
get out their Tally-Ho,†
lick the gummed edge slowly,
stick the paper to their lips, squint at the sky
lay tobacco down the centre, a sacrifice,
pick bitter brown bits off their tongues
tempt the clouds to let it down, tip their lot
a Drum* roll to end the drought.

* Drum: a brand of roll-your-own tobacco
† Tally Ho: a brand of cigarette paper

Frost

Winter wallflowers and wild mustard
make a magenta and yellow bush.
Sweet smell of silage catches
in my throat like ether;
the morning's frost failing
to anaesthetise my senses.

Once we sat in cold bus seats
outside the Bellbrook pub
waiting for the sun to hit
the metal of the double-decker.
Lyall lifted the bonnet,
poured drops from a secret phial.

Ether heated the engine
white clouds of oblivion
seeped gently into the cabin.
Navy tunics and grease spots
in brown paper bags
took on a strange clarity;

through dilated eyes we looked
benignly on this new beauty
and Jenny Larkins knitting
two sleeves on the same needle
in stripes of magenta and yellow
seemed as astonishing as

the blue and red Sydney bus
crawling up the mountain
with its load of stoned
half-frozen kids, singing
'She Loves You'* to the driver's
bobble hat and red-tipped ears.

* 'She Loves You': a Beatles song

Short cut to Cathcart

Double trucks shimmer
wheelless on new road.
We cut the corner back
of Bombala, feel soft tyres
gripping gravel, leave dust
hanging on our exit.

Chimneys without houses
stand in yellow paddocks,
barbecues minus backyards
waiting for a gift pack
of Mitre 10 tools.

Behind cypress windbreaks
new homesteads keep their
heads tucked down into
Hardiplank while
hot northerlies suck at tin.

Dams unplugged, earth's eye
sockets ploughed circular
by walking wool;
eucalypts radiating away
scrabble to keep hillsides still.

Vernie Coles' store is there yet;
weatherboards flaking into
ice cream and petrol.
Anyone under the veranda?
Vernie? Sao biscuits, sacks
of spuds and flour on tick?*

Wooden finger pointing left
gives no clue to cliff-cut track
down which Vernie's stock
once came but we can
almost smell the hessian.
Pump the brakes, try not
to look down – don't want
to get home that soon.

* on credit

Corella farewell

While we hurried for the bus to Canberra
which pulls up opposite Centrelink
you reversed into a pole that props
up the CWA balcony and the crew
in a search and rescue truck
having coffee out of thermos cups
cracked up but their chortles drowned
in the racket from a cloud
of Little Corellas an explosion
of cackles more crass than cicadas
as they climb the cumulus,
careen across Church Street
and crash land in the she-oaks
as the bus floats up the road,
silent until it breathes out
on pressure brakes.

Canberra via CountryLink

Two blowflies got on the bus at Nimmitabel
as the compression doors swish they cruise fat
and yellow up the aisle two women yack
the way from Bega one with a voice that would carry
the motion in any committee not loud almost refined
persistent as a dentist's drill without the variation
when it hits a nerve the other lower and aggressive in
agreement *well that's right too what did she expect*
don't pause to swat they could drone for Australia
top marks for duration and consistency in tone
driving all those condemned to listen to who said what
and how wise and perceptive they both had been
to move to the back of the bus a separation of
dandelion heads who use the trip to earbash captives
from those who plug in to iPods or study their book so fiercely
they could bore a hole in the page while the boys with baseball
caps on back to front and the girls with pierced navels
curl bare feet up on seats and mobile* at five k intervals
just going through Bunyan Bredbo Michelago I'll call
you when we get to the hospital and smile secret smiles at
I heart u texts electronic beeps and gurgles an orchestra
of intimacy for all that the bus can still hear snatches as
the shaved necks and white curls come together in conspiracy
I told her she ought to have known you can't
get away with velveteen at fifty it spread to her liver
look at the udders on those cows a sudden desire
to own an iPod plug in be deaf to the conversation
up the front fly bounces off the Sudoku with two
eights in the same column and sits concussed
on a window long enough to be sent to blowie heaven

it remains a smear on the puzzler's failure while
the Bloody Monaro blurs by and we pray that its mate
will gravitate down the throat of Madam President
who sideways on bares her teeth and enunciates
you never put vanilla in an anzac everyone knows that

* mobile here is a verb meaning to use one's mobile phone

Maybe Street

1

The owner's son drove us
to a garden where the house had gone
it's tombstone a chimney and grate.
Orchard skeletons black against
winter grass and old double daffodils,
petals bursting out of buds,
lime green through age, not yellow,
bulbs split and spread by the plough.

He watched, eyes quick, leaning on
his flash car, you laughed together
as we picked, his girl and I,
bitter milk from the stems ran up our sleeves.

Took us back to the mill cottage,
three rooms and a lean-to;
a seven-foot Canadian and the woman
who came up to his waist chucked out
the week before we moved in for
sticking logs into the grate, propping
the other end on a chair out into the room:
the walls were black from their burnings.

Snowflakes fell through the hole in the wall
hissing as they hit the bathwater;
Canadian's wife would squat in the copper,
fire bubbling beneath, boiling her backside,
I'd have climbed in there too if I'd fitted.

She worked with her man at the mill;
when I walked silently between the stacks
to steal loose bits of four by two* I could see
the long and the short of it, shapes in a blizzard,†
one each end of a log. Tug free a piece glued by frost,
retreat to the kitchen, push it in the fire box,
sit the other end on a chair.

Burns on my arms where the stove kissed
me as I pushed pans to where the iron glowed red
flesh sizzled, stuck to the top, bubbles on skin
then peeled away like rings of sunburn.
Doctor traced them with his fingers when
he took my blood pressure, thought I was a battered wife
looked at me with soft-eyed concern.

A bucket of bulbs coated in clay left on the doorstep.
Dig a hole in the cold soil under the hedge,
place them in gently side by side, like buryng dead kittens.

See the crane go by, front wheels off the ground,
the Canadian and his wife hanging onto
the fender to balance the log the owner's son
is swinging, his eyes on the window where
I make a hole in the condensation to see him wave.

* a standard timber size, in inches
† they are lost in a cloud of industrial sawdust

Came back once; mill closed, cottage gone,
bulldozed by the boss after his son
was impaled by a timber leaping from the belt.
Dead before he hit the sawdust, wouldn't have felt
a thing, others said.

Drove around, up through yellow paddocks,
Looking for the tombstone chimney
and a field of lime-green daffodils.

2

She came with the first blowfly
sat on the good chair and told me
I needed a pram mine would not be
big enough for two I could have one
her last had grown out of
and a table for the kitchen too.

Her man delivered a chrome and black
carriage smelling of plastic and puke,
a laminex table with rusty legs
its top a mouldy mottled green;
and a fat-bellied puppy thrown in.

When she was born, she said, (a litany)
they did not think she would live –
head the size of an orange, knitted it
a doll's bonnet, wrapped her in sheep's wool
placed her in a shoebox shoved her
in the warmer under the stove.

From the blue-red mottle of her skin
I thought they'd left her there too long
but that was just the Bombala kiss
women bloom early there, faces too close
to the fires they stoke all winter.

I scrubbed the pram and covered tabletop
in stick-on scarlet poppies, pushed the pup
away from my daughter's rusk,
set a bowl of japonica in the window,
a sign of faith that spring would come.

They want $20 for the pram, you said,
over chops and mash. Half a week's wages –
What are they going to do, repossess it?
We'll need it though, I'll slip him ten.

Puppy hiccupped a bundle of spaghetti
that uncoiled slowly on the settee.
I shut my daughter in the bedroom
swept the obscenity up with face averted
scrubbed with Dettol, pushed pills down
the dog's throat could never touch it again.

She brought me a blue plastic bath
when my son was born I sat it on
the transformed table wondered when
we'd be brought to book.
His head is big enough she said
could be a grapefruit I thought
or possibly a shaddock.*

When we moved to the coast her man
had space for a load, made out
there was a ten dollar note in the space
under the dresser *that's your wages then*
wiped the grin off his face.

I'd like my table back, she said, sniffed
when I gave it with baked-on poppies where
I'd set hot pans. I'd have returned
the dog but it went to live at the baker's;
I'd see it waddling along full of day-old bread
when I wheeled the kids down the street.

I was thinking of her the other day
when I stood in front of the oranges.
Was her baby head a Valencia
tinged with green, a great glowing Navel,
or a pippy mandarin, sour as buggery.

* a large citrus fruit

3

Sometimes my mother rang
Perce and Mary's next door.
Perce would come around,
she sounds awful sick
I picked up the phone
recognised the thickness
of sherry in her voice
missed the desperation
that made her think
I had anything to give.

We were separated by
Big Jack Mountain
and the lack of a car
in miles about thirty
down the goat track
but I might as well
have been on Mars
she spoke from her misery
in the school house
I answered from my exile
on Maybe Street.

The blaze from the furnace
lit up my nights; by day
the sound of the saw
a whine in my vertebrae
she imagined she could
gain salvation through
my daughter in Bombala
and the grandchildren too.

4

Perce's Great Dane
stuck its head over the fence
drooped into the pram
laid its jowls in my daughter's lap
she clasped the huge head
wrapped her fat legs around it
looked up at me and shouted with joy
I was reflected in this happiness
my smile a reverse of folds in
the dog's brow, its innate gentleness
a quality I would never possess.

My brother got a lift over the mountain
came to make some money on the mill
we gave him a bed on the settee
after a week of stacking logs and sweeping sawdust
he took his yellow pay packet down the street.
Pushing groceries from Permewans in the pram,
we followed him back up
laughed at the plastic bag on his arm
reckoned he'd blued it on Drum*
and motorbike magazines
but he showed us a pair of grey school trousers
Mum's putting patches on the patches of my other ones.

That night the bedroom door crashed
against the wall and he stood there,
naked in the night horrors, screaming,
you took him by the hand, led him back,
laid him down made soothing sounds
until his crying died away.

* wasted his money on tobacco

We could have walked to the hospital
but we borrowed the foreman's car
when pains came two minutes apart
The doctor held up, cord still attached,
a boy with brow as lined as the dog's
against a backdrop of burning stacks,
seen through the window of the labour ward,
his hands held up in supplication,
spine arched against the Hell of birth,
hot northerlies and a timber mill on fire.

In the Clearing

Concerning the so-called Forest Wars in south-east Australia, mostly
in the 1980s and the 1990s, but still smouldering today

It's small, shot from above in black and white
a handmade house in the clearing –
toys dropped when the players were called
into the back of the four-wheel drive.
When the road went through there was talk
of a man who had a tank in the hills;
he planned on blasting loggers' machinery
but mostly dreadlocked kids in their teens
dryads with sarongs or holes in their jeans
walked out of the trees after doing a stint
sat on planks in a fork, high on dacka –
dreamy they dodged blue and red lights.

Leo asked me to go there then; his beard
made him look like Methuselah.
He loaded us into the tray of his ute;
we clutched the sides, tried not to slide out
as it ground up and through the old growth
to where the road would go along the ridge –
my brief to shout to the children aloft
don't you worry about falling off or *what
do you say to the wives of timber workers*
and *when are you going back to uni?*

Answers drifted down through the leaves;
on a breath of patchouli a pale face peered,
said at night she tied herself to her mast
in case she dreamed and rolled; she sat
and listened to wild pigs forage below
boars gashed each other with their tusks
she was glad she was not on the floor –
the rope (pulled up) her umbilical cord.
She threw it down, invited me to climb –
I never could do ropes at school
and got dizzy on a ladder's third rung;
unlike this slender arborealist's
my courage had never been put to the test.

Back at the house Leo's tufty-heads hid
from cameras and questions behind
their mother's hippy skirt, extensions
of golden chrysanthemums on the cloth.
She wiped their noses with it, laughed,
pushed them from her, cut them slabs;
bare feet pattered on the veranda boards
they jumped into the dirt, mouths stopped
by leathery bread stained with dark red jam,
shrieked at emus pacing like warders that scared
them into dropping as much as they ate
– *grow wilder than blackberries, feral kids!*

The fight for the forest was lost on the ridge;
sitters dislodged and taken to court – the tank
remained a myth. My story's guts were edited out
so the paper didn't cop any flack, and regrowth
too spindly to scale grew over the track.
Leo's woman left him, his liver packed in;
for a while some hung on at the commune
until the creek ran dry – now only those
who can start pumps and generators
live like frontiersmen away from the law
take their families, shotguns and trucks
to reclaim the shacks and live on the edge.

Paddy wagons won't bump into the dense
scrub for rifle fire, a sharp cry cut off
or the smell of a bong; there is a satellite dish
on the roof but recycled windows show only black.
In the clearing there is still the sense that anything
can happen here at Pericoe; the dogs whine
uneasy at the motor's hum, barking when
at last neighbours come, switch it off
their faces blanched as they dial triple 0.
A battered chrome and plastic swing looks
as though the children have just slid from it
the absence of their play immense.

The Ladies' Association

The ladies meet and plan dances schoolmaster's wife lifts her pen as secretary Joyce takes the chair donations are two tins of salmon two pounds of tomatoes six of sugar a pound of tea eight loaves of bread and instead of meeting in the filtered light of Edith's lace curtains they splat March flies sit in the shade of the bridge timbers talk about having Arnold as MC change into swimmers behind bushes dip in the deep brown hole Anne comes out in a pink bikini makes the eyes water

or a barbecue at the foot of the mountain when the cold air makes the blowies dopey mutton chops with bits of fleece hanging on burning wool and smell of fat floating through the tree ferns Beulah will donate a doll in a pink knitted dress and Mrs McChroskie a bottle of wine for the spot prize Mrs Dorothy P will investigate the cost of corned roll at the Co-op and the jumble sale brought in six dollars and seventy-five cents

Devonshire supper for the Easter dance will be easier tins of biscuits broken crunchy with sugar bits for the kids and a mass rising of scones wood smoke drifting down the valley whose will be the highest instead of heaters for the hall a new urn'd be good give the straw broom to whoever's not in the gossip round its steam

ladies take a plate of sandwiches no baked beans or spaghetti please for the May dance and then again in June a raffle Mrs Jack donated custard powder and Josie a bottle of sauce three jellies from Eunice and a tin of beetroot from Mrs Ap tickets three for 20 cents junior spot prizes boys and girls family tickets a dollar too much nobody'll come

The ladies hear a death knell in the Mersey beat and cars that take the kids to the coast but as the chill creeps down the mountain Edith's husband is asked what materials would be required to modernise the kitchen twenty dollars will buy a lot of timber and a sink for the hall the schoolmaster's wife has resigned well they only ever gave her the broom maybe they should have let her wash up sometimes

Mud bricks

The family fills the concrete mixer's belly
with dirt, straw and water;
lets it slosh and slap
until it's the right consistency to pour into moulds
bottomless bread tins with handles wetted to slide
off the bricks very satisfying this for builders
ranging in age from twelve to forty-three
mud pies for grown-ups but not for me
designated mover of bricks dried out enough
to be turned, stood on their sides to air and harden,
or stacked ready for the real work.

Gauging when to lift and not be left with crumbled dirt
is an art unrecognised my satisfaction must be that every soft
brick raised carefully and pressed to my chest for support
has the gentle imprint of my bust

this house will be nurtured,
as the mud brick makers have been,
by my breasts.

Tin can craft

Crocheted tea cosies, coat hangers
macraméd in emerald green
dolls with neon orange nylon
sitting over tissue boxes or do
their perfect plastic bottoms
melt on teapots, orgasmic Barbie?

I once knew a woman who made
pincushions out of empty baked bean tins.
The lid, left hinged, padded
and prettily pink in gingham and white
broderie. Every fete and fundraiser was
marked by Daphne's tin can echidnas
when she died I expected her daughter
to put a fresh one on her grave every week.

Where is the museum for toe covers, dog
coats, patchwork tubes vomiting plastic
bags? Towels appliquéd, embroidered, edged
into scratchy redundancy? Knitted plastic,
nylon bright – the workings of women who
made do, went without, colour hungry;
crafted with skill, just missing the mystery.

Neighbours

I like the woman next door she
throws back chalky-white dog turds
before we know we've lost them
they bounce in my perennial border;
the town dogs, recognising
their own dirt scorn my patch
and squat on her busy Lizzie.*

When our rooster roused the street
at three a.m. four nights in a row
she sent the health and building
man around to chat about putting
a bin over the bird at bedtime.
We took our tea and scones outside;
she watched, curtains twitching,
as we plotted a peaceful chook run.

Coming upon my scrambling rose
pushed back from her fence so
that it fell against the fig tree
I knew she'd done it to help me
collect the sweet pink petals
and I put my potpourri bowl
where the scent would reach out
and finger her nostrils tenderly.

* *Impatiens walleriana*, a small flowering plant

I'd like to thank her for all these
little kindnesses but when I see
her pushing her baby on the street
she ducks into shop doorways or
hides behind the Judas trees.
At night I hear her crying to
'The Dark Side of the Moon'. I must do
something really nice soon
for the woman next door.

Coconut slice

trish love turned up on the veranda with a coconut slice she said it was a coconut slice we wouldn't have known, it was three layers of brown stuff

dad never thought much of slices he said they were neither a cake nor a biscuit give him a good sally lunn* any day and we didn't know trish we'd only ever seen her rounding up garth's cattle on a motorbike so we wondered what she wanted

after she came so did others we never said he'd gone but the word had got around and they all brought something – cakes with bits of burnt date or walnut poking out or split scones with lemon butter stuck to glad-wrap or they clutched posies of january geraniums or arum lilies it wasn't even the funeral why were they bringing flowers

don't you go putting arum lilies on me when I'm dead he said *I don't want those gloomy old things on my chest* he could see them growing out the front of colin's house three clumps holding up the veranda heads neon cones climbing out the dark leaves when he was dying all he could do was sit there looking at them it was like they couldn't wait to get over the road and sit on him

* large sweet traditional English bun

some of the women stopped there and pulled some out to add to their bunch before they got to our house juice dripping down the copy of the news they'd dipped in the water bucket then they wrapped foil around that pulled it together with a creased ribbon, one someone gave to them when the last person at their house died

where will we put all the flowers said mum we dragged boxes of vacola jars out red rubber seals melded into their rims stuck the geraniums and lilies in there were climbing roses too they shed their petals faster than we could sweep them away they were the sort of roses that scramble over banks or hide the rabbit holes at graveyards

the kelpie got sick of barking at the next lot coming up the bank we put their cakes and slices and scones on plates and fed them those and they sat spilling coconut crumbs down their fronts talking to each other about the drought and other people who had died or would die soon and we sat in the kitchen and waited for them to go away

No reward

Under the mountain
blackberries scramble
to cover the house Mum
kept tidy till she died
and the renters moved in
let her pot plants dry out
did up bombs* in the paddock
burnt weatherboards in the fireplace
one let her ex sleep on the veranda
took rent for the dog's bed
forgot to pass it on to us but

When he held up the bank
in town he took a chrome-green
Charger from the paddock wrapped
an elastic bandage round his face
and went in with a sawn-off
chucked the barrel over the back
of Mum's old shed the one
wisteria was winding through
lifting the boards apart and up

* old cars

Teller handed over the Cannery
wages the ex went back to the pub
paid up his tab shouted the bar
settled his bill bought up big at the store
cartons of Benson & Hedges Extra Mild
ready-cooked chooks takeaway chips paid
with cash spilling notes over the counter.
Where'd you get the money mate?
Robbed a bank, what d'you think?
That's him always good for a laugh

On the radio *road blocks are in place on the*
Princes Highway police are stopping
and searching all traffic crossing
the border but have as yet no leads
to the identity of the Eden Bank robber
the weather will continue mild and sunny
in the daytime but frosty at night

I asked my brother to cut back
the wisteria and save the shed
he thought it was easier to knock
it down tossed split boards
under the plum tree left the
copper standing in the corner
came across the rusty barrel
nearly tossed it in the blackberries

thought to do the right thing – he'd
been in town when the sirens went.
What's going on mate?
Some bastard's robbed the bank.
Get much?
Nah – just the Cannery wages –
Shit! 8,000 bucks!
No KFC or videos with the groceries
for the employees this week.

Sergeant's face impassive
as the piece of rusty metal
lies between them he puts it
in a plastic bag
ties a big tag
evidence
lets my brother leave
later
two collar-proud detectives
knock on his door ask him
where he was on that day
when he says he was near
the scene they show him a shot
of who they think the robber is
squint from him to the pic

It does look like you, his wife admits
but the Adam's apple is all wrong
and you don't have that many zits
my brother wants to say *it isn't me*
can't speak he's struggling with
a giggle in his gullet
wouldn't laugh if I was you mate
grunts the tec* from Wollongong
armed robbery they throw away the key

Why would I hand the barrel in if I'd done it?
Search me mate crims do stupid things
Might as well bite the bullet

dredges his brain
to think of the name
of the hobo who sleeps on
the dog bed out the front
of Mum's old place
they search the house and
find six thousand
tucked into a rathole
in the floorboards under a bed
our little sister used to sleep in

* police detective

traced to a Gold Coast Motel
the ex comes quietly he never
had any ammo anyway
my brother's released
from custody and the threat
of an ID parade with faces wrapped
in elastic bandages not covering
zits and Adam's apples; asks

what about a reward you'd
never have got him
or the money back if I
hadn't bought that barrel in

ask the bank say the cops
ask the cops says the manager
we are under no obligation
asked his honorable member
who looked out the window
said he had no jurisdiction

My brother went back to clear up the shed
and wisteria found a pile of credit
cards the police had missed
with different names embossed
scattered among the snow-in-summer*

* a small white flowering plant, *Cerastium tomentosum*

looked at the mountain
looking down at him tossed
them in the blackberries
identities
lost for ever in
Monaro weeds and frost

Old

'Old' comes from an Indo-European word that means to nourish.
Ancient manuscripts spell it 'Eald'. The word 'World' was once
spelled Wereald – This nourishing place, so full of eald.

Last night came close to a frost
loosening the leaves on the honey myrtle.
Uneasy summer passes, girls slender
as asparagus shiver, cover up and peer
elf-like over layers of Cotton On;*
their defences uncurled by each
sharp night and dewy morning
every turning of this old world;

while I pull out pilled hand-knits
stump along in gumboots to inspect
tangles of long grass and vines,
stub toes on Queensland Blues,
marvel at Orange Japs – a string
of lanterns weighing down the wire
emerge from not-quite-icy mist
that weathers skin, grows calluses,
like the pumpkins', impervious.

* a clothing brand

The cycle is complete, rounded
as I gather up the crop, provide
against another winter, my world
grounded and filled with old.
Beyond the call of fashion, I form
a block against coming storms,
foster the tender who might
snap in a gale, or need to be wrapped
in hessian against a heavy frost.

The Swing

There's a place along the river where
cars pull in beside the alluvion
under casuarinas that suck up minerals
so their trunks are four linked arms around
and the first branch needs a cherrypicker
or a monkey to get up there.

Somebody did go out on a limb;
tied a tow rope for those who want to
swing out over the golden water, letting go
when there's enough below to land in,
dipping with a delicious inner drop
back to the bank if the flow has stopped.

Sometimes when I go by with the dogs
kids party under the canopy; spill from sedans
older than they. Girls flushed with
alcopops, rings glinting from tongues
sit in tree root seats as the boys
leap out with Tarzan whoops.

Slender as wild bamboo these girls
innocent in their tipsy pleasure
swaying over to pat the dogs.
There is always one who takes the dare
swings higher than the boys, afterwards
they sit with hair slicked to scalps, talk
rises with sweet smoke and mosquito hum.

Told my grandsons about the swing;
we waded the stream, dogs splashing ahead.
At first I thought the ribbons and cellophane
catching the sun were KFC debris; chips
and chicken bones sprouting from takeaway
seeds – I once found a scattered settee,
split cushions spread through the weeds.

Mounded against the trunk fake flowers
under a print-out photograph smudged
with last night's condensation, as though
from crying; eyes that knew enough at sixteen
not to want to stay alive. The rope was gone –
untied and removed, she was the last high flyer.

A casuarina had its bark hacked out
almost in a ring – angry, red cuts
that just fail in their attempt to kill the tree
from which she swung. As the dry year
draws on and the flow in the river dwindles
the roots suck deep and the wind
soughs through the needles.

Autumn storm

An explosion in
tangled reeds as the blue wren
and his harem feed.

Wattlebirds feud, swoop
low over the ground; pursued
now the pursuer

Gold quota for bees
their quest for pollen quenched
in sasanquas'* hearts

In late autumn heat
insects swarm; clouds for the storm,
That blots out the sun

Dog stumbles, ears twitch as
kangaroos thump in the mist;
lame, she can still watch

Today we heard black
cockatoos their wail carried
on a rain cloud's back

* *Camellia sasanqua*, a large flowering bush

My mind doesn't feel
the climb as I walk the rough
track thinking of rhymes

Smoke drifts to meet us
our breath catches in the chill
light glows from the house.

The swallows leave

This time again; trees
stripped in autumn gales, silhouettes
against a pale moon

Frost crisp underfoot;
bring the blue pot of fragrance in,
lemongrass for soup

Leaves scrape the deck, blown
like ragged scraps; inside, the fire
warms me to poetry

Outside you dig holes
deep for two bare sticks, their buds
pledge magnolias

Yesterday the sky
was filled with swallows;
today they have flown.

Cracking nuts

your outline is hazy against
a fountain of wisteria as you sit
on the edge of the concrete
bringing down a hammer

a cold front on the Fleurieu
blows petals over the patio
almond trunks blacken in the rain

when the clouds roll out to the Bight
cars continue to crawl past the sign
offering a rural setting
with glimpses of the sea

we cover the septic pump
with a pot of hen and chickens
fit locks on the laundry door
confound the cats with new closures
so the agent can have a key to exchange

taking nuts from the box
we have a crack   alternate
between being too gentle
so the split will not separate
or crushing the kernel

you seem so close we can
almost see you hear the clean
break of long practice
your cat is curled in your lee

it's the last betrayal leaving you there
a half smile of surprise
at our departure on your uplifted face
the hammer poised for the last time

Separation 1

Waking up alone
no clink of kitchen cups to
tell me where you are

Sweeping the front steps
I prepare the house for guests
who may never come

Meaningless without
a voice: people talk on a screen
with the sound turned off

Midday mailman shoves
flyers from the Asian Pearl
into my letterbox

Over Biamanga
drone slices the afternoon:
three o'clock plane

Upward rush of wings
a thousand sacred ibis rise
over the lagoon

Feeding fires from the
pile you split; will it last
until your return?

This was the time when
doors slammed, bags thumped, chatter flowed
children home from school

Shut in the chickens
against foxes; soft talk from
the dark corner perch

Piecing together
cranes, kimonos, chrysanthemums
symbols in a quilt

Lamp extinguished, still
my bedroom glows; the moon hangs
framed in the window

From the water, night
watchmen scream at predators:
plovers defend nests

Light brings cat, dogs
and hope to my bed – is this the day
you set out for home?

While you were away

The poem describes fruit bats, a large bat also called a flying fox

Half a ragged moon shows over
the hay-bale wall, a cover for
great shapes that weigh down
the strawberry guava tree
screeching at each other
and then at us as we go by
reaching for the choicest bits
membranes let through light
as they flap, heavy with fruit
you can feel what it takes to rise
they snap the plant in lift-off
and anchor themselves to the figs
which they tear leaving wart
medicine seeping from the twigs
maybe here and there a piece
of torn pink flesh I shine
my torch into their foxy faces
so they scream down at me
and lift up and away across
the gash of moon, black
harpies skimming back
across the lagoon, the dog
shrinks away from the sight
and together we go in
and hide from the night.

Witness

Looking for October's orchids
I climb down to the creek bed
and find indigo bush growing
where the pool was

once I knew where to place
every footfall which rocks
would give or roll wrenching
a tendon so you could hear it
like a branch cracking

drought has made it a flower
garden and the years of not wanting
to see no water have made me hesitant
but like old friends I find two rocks
leaning together over a third
where the water cascaded icy cold
on its way down Cow Bail from the plateau

this was our bath our shower
we'd dip heads under and feel
our brains go numb our minds
singing like crystals
our daughters ran naked up the path
to the cabin bodies white and slim
between the ghost gums

here is the rock that makes
a sun bed tilted at the right angle
to watch water dragons creep
from where the wild fig split
the rock face
they dance on a slant
small lizards reposition
around the larger one playing out
a ritual commonplace to me then
now many years
since I have been a witness

the orchids have not flowered yet
spilling like cream over the great rock slope
cushioned with moss on which I sat alone
and cried out because the shock of
cold water could not numb the loss

the cry echoed off grey surfaces
and was picked up by black cockatoos
who knew the rocks had heard it all

Colour charts

Squares of colour
shining out of
frames
each christened
by an artist or a poet
or the stitcher
of a cathedral
window quilt
calico is on the chart
burnt sienna
terracotta
umber too
In the landscape
I am painting out
the shades become
bleached cow bones
rising like the frame
of a Viking ship
out of the cracked silt
at the bottom of the dam;
dried wombat skin
as the trim
its long teeth
curved as a prow
an accent called
buttercup
in the quilt.

Separation 2

You have been gone too long
the split wood is all burnt
and farmers turn tall weeds into hay.

Although spring came early
with hot blasts and thunderstorms
this morning my bare feet ached
with frost on the grass.

Wisteria uncurled in your absence
reached out and grabbed anyone
who tried to pass. I thought each day
to slash it and then you came back
and in two minutes the way was clear
secateurs unused in my grip.

There are words I should have said
that will not now pass my lips;
after the first betrayal they never come
as easy and time has hardened this
silence but still the cold space
in my bed is better warmed
by you than anyone else.

Changes

Biamanga is a mirage
hovering over the deck;
golden skinks burn their feet
as they shimmy across the slats
to drop into a black plastic
underworld, out of the heat.

The full moon lifts
on warm evening air
framed by the spotted gum
and the mountain;
casts an amber light
in a grey and red tinged sky
not so much a delight
as a warning.

The mountain has trapped
low cloud this morning;
droplets a veil over all,
steam ramped up until
it becomes a shroud
under which we sweat.

Something sighs,
whether it's us or clouds
it's hard to say but a cool breath
precedes a growl and a crack
then gusts set the trees
aslant, rain comes in lines
like a Japanese print.

It pools in deck oil
swirls in rainbows
reflecting the flashes
that split the sky.
We count the seconds
between fork lightning
and crashes
which synchronise
over the house.

In post storm brilliance
low-flying pelicans
cruise over the way;
dog-walkers duck
as the birds come down
with a prolonged splash
where cows grazed yesterday.

Bumper harvest

Bound in kikuyu, feral cucumbers
are discovered when we stub
our toes on them some prickly
and etched by snails others studded
as though to titillate, gross
engorged and yellow from sucking
up dew and weakened sun I know
their insides will be hollow.
Their English cousins, gently forced in
frames, delivered to the kitchen
pale green and premature
were sliced wafer thin
between soft white bread and butter;
everything is twice the size and obscene
out here Mum used to mutter.

as if we didn't have enough
neighbours dump bulging plastic
bags by the door when we are out
there's not much to be done with a glut
of cucumbers; Greek salads pall and
even the chickens are sick of tzatziki.
I toss them on the compost, watch
them explode in a final mess
of pips, pulp and bitterness.

Almond blossom

In winter we close into ourselves
the coming spring too much of a push
green shoots seem removed from us.
Outside the almond tree is too stiff
to bend with the gale coming down
from the Monaro, lichen stirs like hair
on its silver wood yet against snow
clouds single blossoms glow, have
their moment before the final snap.

Gifts

You walked to the empty house
past piles of somebody's life
and gathered pale papery jonquils
their scent sweeter than rotting carpet
but still with a hint of putrescence
the frost hadn't quite killed

I had asked you for the white japonica
from behind the cabin and also the red
growing where once there were two
houses, then one, then a shed
now just this stand of scarlet
on bare brown spikes beside the road
lit by a winter sunset

You cut the tough stems with secateurs
risked losing an eye on those long thorns
brought in sprays that looked like escapees
from a Japanese scroll then limped
off to bathe your wounds and apply balm

I filled the vases, tried not to put them where
they would inflict further harm. Your gift
to me of winter blooms is more
than I expect these years; you left
me long ago but a memory lingers
and you still return, at dark,
to a fire and the warm smell of food
my gifts to welcome you home.

Galahs

As the light streaks with red and grey
I sit on the soft chair on the deck
and let wine heighten and dull my senses
then the galahs come screaming in
to settle in next door's gums they flash
fragments of sunset falling into tree tops
fledglings wheezing at parents, females begging
from males, cock birds raising crests
defending their roosts then starting up
as if at a signal, squawking off to carry on
the cacophony to other trees in the park

I sip and wonder at how the mob
understands the evening chaos
falling into family groups
secure until sunup starts
the discordant urgency again.
When the bagpipes subside into gurgles
which sometimes boil over as
flapping squabbles in dark branches,
and fewer shapes fly overhead,
mosquitoes begin to bite.
That's my signal to flap around the kitchen,
banging saucepans, tripping over the cats,
look for my mate coming home
settle for the night.

Orange trees

Released the tree from its burden
fingers cold picking oranges crisp
with frost the knife crunches on ice
as it slices them in two. Squeezed,
juice comes colder than from the fridge
we drink the essence of citrus thick
with pulp feel the shiver all through
as the sharpness hits our core.

In late winter the Seville tree
gave us fruit tart enough to take
the lining out of our mouths. Boiling
with sugar could not sweeten
the distillation of frosts,
gales and hard ground, and genes
predisposed to marmalade.

After spring rains a tree
barren for half a decade
was heavy with oranges
of such lusciousness we
feasted for weeks our skin
always sticky so that wasps
tried to drink the juice from us.

Now a cold snap knocks a crop
from the third tree which has neither
the bite of the Spaniard
nor the nectar of the Navel
but we will eat pale-fleshed
segments that pull apart
on pithy threads until
the season passes.

Voices

Starting up, the old dog hears a voice
calling from a long way off, familiar.
Some day soon she will stagger down the
path it beckons, head lifted to meet
the warmth of hands she once knew well
and words of love she'd die to hear.

We sit, she and I, straining to hear
the murmuring of those who speak
in other dimensions, above the stringybark's
dry grating, the creek in fresh – voices
tumbling over cress-bittered granite
laughing softly in moss-sponged beds.

Who'll go first, the dog or me?
Beyond the locks of stiffened limbs
sloughing off our musty bodies
quickening to half-forgotten yearnings
leaping gladly in the morning's long grass
to embrace the final recognition.

Last walk

We turned in from the beach where
we always did through a veil of fine rain.
Heavy drops fell from the banksias;
behind us waves crashed, black
cockatoos rose screaming,
extensions of the dark wetness,
lightning flashes on their tails.

I could sense you would not get
to the end of the track although
you knew every step and how
much you would have to put into
making your body work one more time.

Sun pierced the veil making a pathway
of light; I turned to see if you were still
with me but you had stopped, absorbed
in the prints of those who had gone before.

When you fell I wanted to
leave you there on the path
you knew in the sun
and the light and the clear
fresh smell of old friends
and newly fallen rain.

Withdrawal

the librarian looks like Barbie on
stiletto heels hair spiked in auburn silver
and magenta over tiny face possum eyes behind
batwing glasses a name like a beauty salon
behind her on a desk small pelts
protected in plastic bags or maybe
Bill Oddie's sporrans plotting escape
laughing at the Goodies* is a long way
from the fluorescence of the oncology
unit as the lights shimmer
on rainy streets outside
Barbie frowns as she tucks floating
strands into an Ena Sharples† net
can she remember Coronation Street
pulls a dead animal over her client's
skull pushing a multi-frown
wave fashion down her forehead
combs the springy synthesis
tweaks with perfumed dedication
raises an eyebrow in question
at the grim stranger in the mirror
who is unconvinced insists they try
another this time she is a '60s Cilla Black
no one will know it's me she cries

* a UK comedy TV show with Bill Oddie
† a character with a hair net in the long-running British TV show
Coronation Street

that could be a good thing the librarian replies
and pulls out a silver highland terrier
with bouncing curls a gleam of corrective
zeal in her magnified eye
a withdrawal is made taken away in a bag
with comb and shampoo she'd like to
release it into the wild but she's promised
to return it when her own hair grows back
even so she can see her wig scurrying down
the drain to hide for as long as it takes

Downtown

There's a goat outside Centrelink
its lips curled in a sociable leer
one foot in a Gloria Jean's* takeaway cup

The wheelie bin outside
Café Evolve smoulders
passers-by pour on bottled water

A magpie is chivvied from
the fresh food section at Coles
and perches on the enchiladas

A car with Mexican plates† slots in
tight parking spots the occupants find
they can't open their doors to get out

After the bamboo forest‡ is bulldozed
a wombat turns up in a Sattler
Street garage looking for a burrow

A blue-tongue didn't make it across
the Museum intersection:
flattened into street art.

* a coffee shop franchise.
† a car from south of the border, ie: Victoria.
‡ a large weed patch by the river in Bega, used by many for many
purposes for many years

We will always live by the sea, we said

Written for Anna and Bob's fiftieth wedding anniversary

it is hot in the tiny room
we can hear waves rolling in
washing the sand clean

our bodies make sucking sounds
as we separate and come together again

sunburnt and sleepy
in our summer world, tossed by
breakers, salty scrubbed

as the season swells our skin peels
to a soundtrack – 'Good Vibrations'

city pavements throw
up heat, shop interiors
dark, coolly beckon

won ten dollars in work's sweep
bought a piece of blue brocade

inevitable
this progression from passion
to a wedding dress

a zircon sparkles as much as
diamonds, zenith of my dreams

a full moon lights up
the empty beach too cold now
for midnight walking

friends gather before taking
different roads to the same place

basin moulds groom's cut;
best man barber unaware
wet hair shrinks stooge-like

what is celebration for some
robs others of their sleep

neighbours tap on thin
walls they have to work while we
leave the grind behind

cockroaches temporarily
regain dark spaces we vacate

the bride takes a night train
while the groom and his minders
fill the Morris Isis

which guzzles petrol too fast
single pump store darkly closed

the rabbit man comes by
his ute fur lined with corpses
stops to give advice

light winking from a farmhouse
shots put travellers to flight

more lights – the only
other guests on the road let
the groom siphon gas

the journey continues, punct-
uated by petrol hiccups

in the morning much
excitement – second valley
wedding in ten years

the bell which rang children in
from play hangs silent waiting

conversation rises
outside the school-house magpies
sing the morning in

a neighbour has recycled
peach lace for '60s bridesmaids

white chrysanthemums
from settler's gardens fashioned
a cross for the bride

paper arches over panes
turn a hall into a church

brief panic – flower
girl has arrived bare bottomed
and unrepentant

Dad's long fingers hit the keys
head nods in time to Mendelssohn

Grandfather marches me
between hall benches to where
you wait, dark in suit

I kneel, unable to rise;
Daniele stands on my train

siphoned petrol fumes
linger when the parson says
you may kiss the bride

from homes along the valley
come plates heavy with cream cake

hand embroidered cloths
bleached to hide tiny darns, tied
with silver ribbons

pride of place among gifts
an electric frying pan

school inspector gives
a three-legged cut-glass vase
a wobbly omen

Mum wears a silk rose on her head
that falls askew when she laughs

glasses raised in toasts
Champagne for the head table
present from the Pub

bubble-flushed Grandad rises
makes a speech that no one hears

dust rose with dancing
we were supposed to leave as
the party got going

bumped our way down the coast; car
smelled of old leather and frost

Arctic wind whips up
waves; over the shaky pier
love's out of season

but we need no stove for warmth
not even a double bed

hunger draws us out
to search the grey seafront
whipped by Tasman gales

fish and chips a fitting feast
for universal lovers

storm-raked sand scattered
with spiral shells, we gathered
some with occupants

whelk presence in the car grew
oppressive when brief sun shone

nausea came in waves
sick from love so soon? The child
within me shifted

paper jonquils in a ploughed
paddock look pale in the afternoon

beside an empty
homestead where a fireplace stands
abandoned long ago

we make a home rooms lit by
a red lamp my brothers gave

when ocean gales blew
in that spring, the plastic glow
enough to warm us

one small window allowed us
a stormy triangle of sea.

CPSIA information can be obtained
at www.ICGtesting.com
Printed in the USA
BVHW090320070521
606654BV00007B/1175